Showing Up

poems by

Esther Stenson

Finishing Line Press
Georgetown, Kentucky

Showing Up

for my beloveds

Copyright © 2020 by Esther Stenson
ISBN 978-1-64662-138-5 First Edition
All rights reserved under International and Pan-American Copyright Conventions. No part of this book may be reproduced in any manner whatsoever without written permission from the publisher, except in the case of brief quotations embodied in critical articles and reviews.

ACKNOWLEDGMENTS

Heartfelt thanks to Susan Facknitz, who was my first poetry teacher at James Madison University and ultimately read and encouraged me to submit these poems for publication. Laurie Kutchins also figures prominently in the development of what poetic voice I have. Without her patient and insightful coaching, my first book would never have come into being. Julia Kasdorf and Jeff Gundy further deserve a big thank you for playing a part in encouraging past and present writing endeavors. Thank you also to Bonnie Connelly for her excellent artwork for the cover. Finally, my dear friend Lynne Moir always has time to listen to the worst and the best of what I write. Thank you all!

Publisher: Leah Maines
Editor: Christen Kincaid
Cover Art: Bonnie Kraus Connelly
Author Photo: Jim Bishop
Cover Design: Elizabeth Maines McCleavy

Printed in the USA on acid-free paper.
Order online: www.finishinglinepress.com
also available on amazon.com

Author inquiries and mail orders:
Finishing Line Press
P. O. Box 1626
Georgetown, Kentucky 40324
U. S. A.

Table of Contents

I.

Reunion I. 1
Reunion II. 3
Reunion III. 5
Reunion IV 7
Reunion V. 8
Their Girl 9
A Day with Mom 10
One Week in August 11
Juxtapositions 13
Uncle Jake 14
Uncle Jonas 16
Uncle Norman 18
Uncle Alvin 19
Rock of Ages 20
Letting Go 21

II.

Just Staring 22
Your Love 23
Side Show 24
That Tree 25
The Big Rain 26
Said 27
Labor Day on Loft Mountain 28
Black Friday 29
Mattamuskeet 30
What Matters 31
A Bird 32
Showing Up 33
Museum Afterthoughts 35
Of Words and Walls 36

I.

Reunion I.

Here among the dark-clothed, fully clothed men and women
now gray-haired, once schooled over this still solid plain wood floor,
I, of the youngest—last grade taught here—
wonder what is worthy of remembrance,
what sustained us and nurtured us onward,
our lives fractured by moves to other places,
other ways of thinking ,
other friends and neighbors,
or perhaps sustained by moving on,
or holding on.

Nature Study is first on the men's list of learning
—how it taught them to see the red on the wing
of the blackbird clinging to waving grains,
its nest so finely woven to keep out wind and rain
—how they learned that caring for the earth means
respecting each tiny insect and flower, bird and tree,
understanding that each is necessary
for survival of the whole community
of speaking and unspeaking things.

They remember first settlers and visionaries
from Norfolk who understood that as God made
all the creatures of the field to complement each other,
so each speaker must be respected for the center to hold.
Though no one mentions it, we remember how community began to crack,
beginning with the dark beard who took his own way
without counsel, persuading others in secret.

One somber woman stares at me, perhaps
wondering how Sam's girl came to leave this place,
wondering how I live in a world they can only imagine,
a world far removed from the days
—of cold air slapping my seat in the outhouse,
home of vagrant brown spiders and
a Sears & Roebuck catalog outdated for all but a final swipe
—of running like an antelope chased among the apple trees in the

church yard, now and then picking up a red crisp one for a bite,
or a soft one to aim at one deserving.
—of volleyball and baseball with all, remembering
the day I slammed a hard one into Tom Swarey's tummy,
terrified when he didn't show up the next day for class.

—of single base and prisoner's base, self-conscious of
that tall dark one who held my hand hard enough to make my face flame.
—of the frozen pond among the cedars in Mccomb's field
where I, a skating girl, first poked around a puck,
 pretending to play hockey like the boys.
—of long walks in forested fields to memorize
verse, or gather mushrooms white and brown, ruffled and red
 for my first report on a varied species.
—of hurrying home past the horse stables where
suspendered boys with tongues untamed
flung sweet nonsense at my retreating back.
—of giggling with Mary, or Anna, or Clara
in our cape dresses, neatly pinned.

I don't know what judgments lay behind that dark face,
but one thing I know.
One black-clad woman held me with her face full
of sweet sorrow, as I sympathized in
her husband's sudden passing.
She confided the pain
yet with her gentle voice so quiet concluded:
"Was Gott Tut Das ist Vohl Getahn."*

---

*What God does is well-done.

Reunion II.

The two-room basement school on Barterbrook Road
Never hosted so many unsuspendered boys and pigtailed girls
—offspring of my students grown a bit gray and rounded.
Once , it seems in another life,
their parents pushed swings, pitched balls, swatted balls,
wore holes in shoes playing soccer on gravel,
or looked for bluebirds down the shaded pasture lane
where I'd walk each weekday morning looking for peace
before the buzzer blared, calling class to order.

Lunching around store-room tables, with "my girls,"
menopause was no topic of discussion back in the life-dawn days
when they appliquéd cats and dogs, flowers and boats
for a sturdy picnic quilt while the boys bent over bean "art"
or glued together plastic model cars
and bought the teacher a bear and cub model
to keep her from feeling left out.

The black eyes of one of those boys that
once fastened on mustard-colored salamanders
in a fern-filled terrarium—counting the three each morning
to make sure they were all living—
now turned their burning, quietly downcast,
toward the teacher turned poet,
 declaring he'd never read poems with such voice
that painted pictures in stories that he could understand,
that he wished to possess.
And I, amazed, wondered what calling
this hard-working man might have missed
—or perhaps what far realms of the imagination
this father of seven might open to his offspring
in fertile fields I have never explored.

In this crowd, I am far removed from
the twenty-one year old first-time teacher I once was,
now admiring the still vibrant, still treasuring
lofty hopes for their multitude of young, seemingly serene
in knowing that each day's grace will be given to
bring up their children in "the Way,"
perhaps wondering if their offspring will, like them,
broaden their beliefs down the stream of years
—or gather in stagnant pools.

Who would have imagined that the treasures
taken from these narrow walls, these students,

3

could gain for this once-shy teacher
an entrance into mud huts and ancient palaces,
varied tongues and tastes,
beyond these borders?

Reunion III.

Gathered under strong oak beams
the older Yoders sat on long wooden benches
as the younger ones perched on oblong bales
in the old hay barn on the family farm as
we listened to the virtues of those just passed on,
or long gone, remembering

how young, blond/blue-eyed Annas
had driven his car to Virginia to visit us
—chatting amiably while I, drawn to this cousin,
was milking cows in our three-stall parlor
—how he'd given his wild heart to God
in the weeks before a heavy truck crossed
the center of a rain-slicked highway
and smashed him beyond reviving.

Vigorous Aunt Mary, who said "no" to
my wanderlusting Kanagy uncle,
waited longer than most Yoder women
before she found a stable home for
her uncommon sense and compassion.
She finally said "yes" to a bereft flock
of five young ones and their lonely father
who begat three more and was blessed by many
for her cheerful heart and quilting hands
before cancer claimed her.

Grandpa Yoder, sharp as hidden glass,
reading Scripture by the light of one dim pull-chain bulb
wouldn't allow any of his offspring undue glory
believing "none are better than they ought to be"
with an honesty some called blunt, but not offensive
among the plain-spoken Yoders.

None remarked on the curiosity
shining in his lively blue eyes that drew him
to Buffalo's Pan-American Exposition,
or his yearning to study at Goshen College
tempered by his love for Grandma and
the confines of her father's faith,
a desire fulfilled by some of his children's children
—those silent in the gathered crowd,
uncertain whether the view of God's grace
in the eyes of some, could cover
learned and unlearned, veiled and unveiled.

My father, could he yet speak,
would have poured from his heart
gratitude for a God who reaches still
from the heights to the depths
of all our broken understandings
and perhaps pried loose
a few more faltering tongues.

Reunion IV

"What will you give?" rang out again and again
in the long hall at Penn Valley Retreat
as tables full of Aunt Amelia's treasures:
glass antiques, hand-pieced quilts, tablecloths,
shells from Florida beaches, and yellowed letters
were sold to her Kanagy "beeplin" who would long remember
how she fussed over each one, lavishing on all
her love and kisses as long as she could reach a face.
She would have given her "stuff" all away,
she once declared, but now she
can hardly remember the faces in front of her.

Uncle Ed's girl, Leah, in her deep sadness
told how she lost her daughter, her son-in-law
and babes among eleven lives snuffed out by
one speedster in a truck, talking on his cell phone.
Yet she felt the love of the God her father found
as he sat one day under the shade of a pasture tree,
reading Scripture and asking forgiveness as his Mom
had told him was the real "Way" rather than mere
mouthing of words to an Amish bishop.
For love of his children, Ed refused to hire them out
for winter work so they could fill his own farm
with their mirth and songs when the snow lay deep.
A lover of horses, he was first to bring to
Big Valley the Morgan stallions whose
bloodlines still infuse the proud horses seen
clopping down the Valley roads between
Jack's mountain and Stone mountain,
though few of his children remain.

Cousin Martha, face fair as a full moon,
 remembered how my Yoder cousin
would ask her to accompany him
to the table at wedding banquets in Big Valley,
how she asked him, days before the truck smashed him,
if he would be ready to meet God should he die
—how he paused for a long moment before
Responding, "now I am"—warming her budding
love for this gentle soul days before he died.

Here, we mingled hugs and tears
with our bean soup and moon pies,
savoring each till we would meet again.

Reunion V.

Once again the lefsa lovers return to the lake
where a lone loon trills an ancient welcome
to offspring of Vikings, branches of Luther,
and this one grafted shoot of Menno Simons.

Here, we are all children as we watch
five small flushed faces chase a pied squirrel around
the trunk of an oak till they collapse in tangled giggles,
or we wonder at Johnny's tales of daring treks
in Southeast Asia—adventures he savors
like brewed tea and steamed dumplings.

Like the rising sun, blazing its crimson path
on the lake's crystal mirror,
the strong ones, both young and old,
perform spectacular risings on skis that skim across
the rippled surface while the envious watch
from the solid shores of Leech Lake.
Mother merganser, unruffled,
leads her seven young fearlessly
across unsettled waters in the wake of jet skis.

One moment, the clouds frown and pout,
spew out a slanted storm with white-capped wings.
The next moment, we paddle and swim,
cleanse our tainted lungs with northern Minnesota air
that strengthens our souls for burdens to come.

When darkness drops its quiet mantle,
Jim ignites fallen sticks and branches knowing
that if he builds it, we will come.
Even the two gone gaming return from
that tomb of a casino and join the sacred circle.

As the moon begins to paint its golden path
on the water, we roast marshmallows on
glowing embers and sing boy scout songs,
cicadas keeping their own time
with the rhythmic rise and fall of the waves
while the loon croons his endless love song
like the web of family we continue to weave.

Their Girl

Because I am the girl of "a good daddy"
as Esther Martin said,
I can always go back to Springdale Church
perched on a rise next to grain and hay fields
stretching right across to the Blue Ridge Mountains.
Nearby tombstones bear testimony of other
Martins, Weavers, and Showalters beloved of my father
who began his new life in the Shenandoah Valley,
working among these people after an exhausted World War II
released him back home to his wife and son.
In this church, the warm hands and wide smiles of the living
still bring tears, bridging the years of memories.

Because I am my Mom and Daddy's girl,
we got invited to old neighbors up on the hill
where a massive stone chimney held a strong fire
on that blustery Sunday after church for a dinner
that tasted like the love in Babette's Feast as
Sadie brought out mashed potatoes dripping with brown butter,
batter dipped roasted chicken, creamed asparagus
with eggs and croutons, cream cheese Jell-o topped with
nuts, green salad overflowing with cheese and bacon
—just like Menno and Sadie's wedding feast fifty years ago
in the long cleaned-out chicken house across the fields.

Because I am my Mom and Daddy's girl,
I prepare for Mom a soft-boiled egg,
peel an orange, and pour hot tea to start her day.
I read my Mom a story till she falls asleep
like she used to do, pre-school, for me.
I serve her chicken and dumplings with corn and parsley
as she asks, "have you had your lunch"?
I play "Old black Joe" on my harmonica, and
sing with her of the glory to come.
I wash her back and tend her sore spots
before laying her flat for the night.

Because I am their girl,
I am glad to play my part .

A Day With Mom

The house is quiet
after the ringing, connecting east with west,
after the singing of old school songs with Mom,
after the chopping, the stirring,
      baking and chirring, drinking and cleaning;
after the washing and hanging,
      struggling with banshee winds, whooshing and chilling;
after the banging and pounding of tacks
      to attach thin strips to stop cold air stealing through cracks.

The house is quiet
after the chiming of hours, half hours, and quarter hours.
after the knitting and knotting,
      trimming uneven ends on finished scarf;
after the reading and talking to Mom
      through clean-ups and wash-downs;
after the sweeping and mopping in this old, old house where
      once I was the one lying in my bed ,
      waiting for food from faithful hands.

"Turn about," she said, "is fair play."
And the wind sings and moans
through the silver maples
still standing guard.

One Week in August

On Sunday,
after four years of living in your narrow bed
expanded only by a window full of sky,
and purple finches feeding on sunflower seeds
while black Alex kept guard beneath the silver maple,
the light in your sharp brown eyes
faded from this side of living
into the mystery of the other side.

Monday was like the blur of a worn wiper blade.

On Tuesday,
The earth shook itself like a giant beast,
lumbering across the ceiling,
startling those of us preparing a table
in the sanctuary with our evidence
of your significance.

On Wednesday, your old birthday,
we sang into our sorrow,
remembering how you would wake the house
singing, "Gone are my friends, to a better land I know,
I hear their gentle voices calling, Old Black Joe."
Then we tenderly laid your body to rest
in the red earth beside your only love.

On Thursday,
your spirit hovered about the kitchen as
I slipped pears into jars, snapped beans, and
boiled tomatoes, preserving the goodness
of God's land that you taught me to love.

On Friday,
I performed the sacraments of
mowing and cleaning, cooking,
 and communing with my brother,
your son from afar,
come to help us celebrate your life.

On the weekend,
as we gathered in Pennsylvania and Indiana
to remember the life of our Cousin Irene,
her essence blew up along the east coast,
drenching and clenching, swirling and whirling,
flambouyant and wild as the Holy Spirit

that reached through her into the hearts of many.

Somewhere in the middle of the week,
in the still of a morning half awake,
I heard a whippoorwill sing through the darkness
like the persistent light that
breaks into another new day

Juxtapositions

1.
The sleek blue and white tractor in the car garage
belied the plain long dress topped with
a large white covering on the matron of the house
and her suspendered, bearded husband.

2.
Gray asphalt lending itself to the speed of a track-trained horse
not used to following a funeral procession,
jolted the buggy's on again off again wheels,
finally shattering one of them as my cousins held on,
then stepped out unhurt, awaiting a car to continue their journey.

3.
Inside the plain white meetinghouse among shade trees,
black-clad friends and family of dear cousin Bennie
silently awaited the words of preachers lined
on the long bench in front of the congregation while
a cell phone's ring reminded us that "the world" was lurking.

4.
In the solemn silence, I riffled pages of the *Lieder Sammlung,*
looking for familiar German hymns of my distant youth,
"*O Gott Vater,*" "*Auch Bleib Bei Uns....*"
—only to find that the ancient high German script
had been printed in modern China.

5
In the churchyard, autos and jet black buggies mingled
as we all contemplated the intersections of life and death.

Uncle Jake

Short, thin, with narrow-brimmed hat on his cocked head,
a faint smile crinkling mournful- looking eyes,
he carried a teakettle all the way from Pennsylvania
for my wedding gift, knowing perhaps how much love
must be poured into a life to make it whole
—longing perhaps for the love that seemed
never to reach the brim of his cup.

Still in his springtime, music poured from his upstairs kingdom
as hungry fingers pressed guitar strings or
accordion keys never seen downstairs
where the Amish neighbors, or "the Bishop,"
might show up unbidden like ashes from the wood stove,
except when the moon shone bright on corn shocks,
bringing music and dancing feet to the barn floor
after the corn was husked.

Songs and stories flowed through the endless dishwashing
he shared with his sister Mattie, next to him up the ladder,
while his brothers' teasing, careless taunts gathered
like black crows roosting around the walls of his heart
till one day he closed himself into the refuge of his room for
two weeks, opening only to his mother's daily plates of food.

Later, desperate for a place to newly nest with his young bird
and three little ones, he bought the upper farm from Jonas
but couldn't claim it 'til the renters decided to leave,
while another brother derided him for buying land
he said was doomed to failure.

The walls thickened as he forbade his children
to play with his taunting brother's children—brooding alone
—fearing even God had closed his heart against him.
The moons waxed and waned as the crows flapped and fluttered
around the fortress, no matter that some siblings urged
him to shoo them away—fling open the doors.

He became a quiet shadow to those he faithfully
sheltered and fed—his wife and children—as he
plodded the years with stone feet.

Here and there, among the shadows, he let in rays
of sunshine when he flooded his pond in winter so he could hear
the bling of blades on smooth ice punctuated by the happy
shouts of his youngest mingling, at last, with their cousins.

When his own nest was empty, he took time to show up
at a concert Mattie's girl sang in, miles from his home,
and was beloved by nieces and nephews
who liked his quiet grace among endless words streaming
from the mouths of other aunts and uncles.
Later, he sold Lee some land at the edge of the hemlock grove
overlooking Big Valley, living nearby in neighborly companionship,
sharing rides to the farm show,
lending tools and helping hands.

Finally, his days nearly done, weary of the darkness and
listening to sister Amelia's urgent admonitions to forgive,
a voice in a vision enquired if he was ready to "let it go."

His answer shone round about him the last week
as he declared among the living that
the love of the Lord had overflowed his cup
and was about to lift him right up to heaven.

And the crows flapped away
to make room for the angels.

Uncle Jonas

With snakes writhing on the front steps
and wheelbarrows full of dried chicken poop
to be scooped from the house floors of
the weathered two-story frame house Jonas bought
on the mountain side of South River (1947)
Mollie and the children yearned for their
tamed farm back in Big Valley near cousins and kin.

What was he thinking?

He barely stepped foot inside the Amish Church
in Stuarts Draft before hauling Molly and all
to a nearby Mennonite Church,
first one, then another, until the children felt
ashamed to show their faces one more time
among one more congregation perhaps thinking
"here comes trouble!"

What was he thinking?

With Kanagy wanderlust,
a mind not meant for "the groove,"
he left one day—left Molly and family
to milk the cows and take care of the farm,
cleaned out his bank account
and flew to Israel like his brother Joe
to see where Jesus walked.

What was he thinking?

There among the ruins, the parables,
the dusty desert and blue Galilee,
did he find a different way
beyond the church fights, the cows
and milk checks, reaping the
fat of the land by the river?

One thing we know.

When the rains came hard and fast,
to Massies Mill, Goshen, and many other places,
filling the Tye River, Maury River, the Mississippi delta,
flooding whole towns and rooms with
slimy water and neck-deep muck,
he gathered the young and the strong

to go dig, scrape, wash, paint, and plant
some hope among the hopeless.

Beyond our shores, smiles of Haitians
greeted his jolly helping hand
that created simple solar cookers
where wood had long been scarce,
digging wells, inspiring son and grandson
to continue the treks to Missippi, to Navajo lands
to build strong structures against the elements
and scatter sunshine among the despairing.

For the joy, not mammon,
he invented, and re-invented the
Flippin' Ginnie to hurry along pancakes
for the Mennonite Relief Sale so that others
around the world could eat.
He imagined a silo unloader, but lost
the patent to one who came snooping one day
and finally lost profit on those he did sell
when he released his accounts to others
who betrayed his trust.

What was he thinking?
Perhaps sometimes he wasn't.
Other times? Of others.

Uncle Norman

Perhaps "Punchie" should have been his nickname rather than Naomi's
for all the times he landed a fist into an arm for a quarrel
just begun, or left over from the day before,
sending a sister sprinting to hide in the privy or bedroom closet
till he had to do his chores out in the barn.

But later, as new growth hides scars left on burned land,
so Norman grew a generous heart to help the hurting.

When cancerous Hodgkins came to visit Kore in 1954,
Uncle Norman left his farm and seven young ones in Pennsylvania
to pick up Kore in Virginia and drive him across many mountains
and rivers to Texas for treatment, refusing offers to help pay for gas.

A brother was a brother.

Dave's death drew him many days and nights to help widow Nancy
on her farm with six left to scratch for themselves,
while his own brood struggled to keep their place afloat,
often missing their dad with a big heart but only one body.

He drove loads of hay, like manna from heaven, round and round,
up and down the hills to Alvin for his mountain cows in West Virginia,
one time leaving him a pick-up truck so new
you could see yourself in its shine
—like the glow on Alvin's face when he first laid eyes on it.

When a horse's powerful hoof killed Ed's Quill,
leaving Annie and her two babes alone on their place,
Norm's tender heart brought him one winter day to
their front door with brand new sleds to slide down those Valley hills,
their spirits soaring as the wind slapped their faces.

No hypocrite, he joined a church where he could freely own
new gas-powered machinery to farm his and others' fields,
and buy a car to drive family and kin where they needed to go,
forgiving his daughter for the scratches she left on its new paint .

Norm, as he was called, went beyond the norm
to leave us a definition of generosity
not to be forgotten.

Uncle Alvin Finds His Calling

Standing in the orchard, short-sleeved in tall grass,
tanned, intent on sliding the bow smoothly
across strings held taut by precisely placed fingers
to fiddle out the young love throbbing
in your heart for gentle Annie

You already knew life could be snuffed out young
when you found your best friend Abner
lying on the road—hurled out of his buggy
by a reckless young driver in a soulless car.
He was so young, the music stalled on first verse.

In Annie and her loving folk
you found an interpretation of God's grace
that went beyond buggies and suspenders,
the teasing torment of ten older brothers
and branding of "Bop"—the baby of the brood.

After you and Annie made your vows in Stuarts Draft,
you took cows to Israel to feed Jews hungry after the war
and milked cows for brother Jonas to feed your own.
Hauling feed for Jason Weaver's little peeps, contemplating
what to do with the treasure of life—be it long or short—
you joined Valley View and set your sights further afield.

Raising turkeys in Rockingham's rough fields,
you took time to serve several congregations in song and Word,
letting your music spill with the Ambassadors
onto the streets of Charlottesville, Stanardsville,
and into the summer tent you set up for children
streaming from hills and mountain hollers to hear
stories and songs about your faithful Shepherd.

Finally, your heart set on awakening souls
to the love of their Creator, you answered the call to
West Virginia mountains where young and old, not rich,
found sweet music in the Good News you preached,
lines and tunes still echoing over those mountains
as far as the eagle flies.

Rock of Ages

The bird,
free of the mind's cage
burst into the nursing home air
relieving the burden of quiet
with her strong guttural parrot-like stream
rocking the ages before pulsing into
"boom ba dee dee dum da"!

Aunt Amelia,
crooning out her own "rock of ages"
to the soft strains of my harmonica said,
"who's that?! as she remembered her dad
bellering from his perch on the four-legged wooden stool
or Sunday buggy seat back home.
Then she turned and hollered,
"Sing then, sing"!

An aide,
not singing, strode over to the bird
and tried to mute her song
by poking a pink lollipop between
her puckered red lips,
but the bird screwed up her face
and would not be stilled.
Sing, bird, sing!

Letting Go

The day after the storms,
after news of your passing,
the sun heralds a new dawn,
a clear shining through each raindrop
still clinging to the clothesline,
which reminds me of how we cling to life
—how hard it is to let go
and commit those who have
given us love and laughter
to the mystery of God's grace
which is fresh as the new grass that
brightens the brown spots
on the lawn after rain.

II.

Just Staring

The wind-blown waters of the winter coast
reveal the arch of a dolphin
—no, another—and another—
breaking water just beyond the shoreline
of a good stare from my hotel balcony.
What rich feast invites their rising and plunging
unhurried in these wide waters?

Another morning's stare sees winged torpedos
dropping from height to depth—first a few—then hundreds,
falling like a hailstorm into the sea—these Northern Gannets,
terrifying fish into the safety of blue depths
before flying further out to sea
to rest and rock on waves
after their frenzied feeding.

Ponderous pelicans glide by the shoreline
in orderly formation
avoiding all commotion,
while one lone sanderling patters on the beach
seeking smaller prey.

The wind whips up the cold waters
and chills my open face,
but it cannot wipe off the wonder.

Your love

Is in the glow of fire-red strawberries
sweetened by sunshine.
and is reflected in the plump and purple
of dew-kissed blueberries.

It is in vermillion ruffles of the
late-blooming petunia reflecting the plumeage
of the rose-breasted grosbeak
catching at a corner of my breath.

It is in the tumbled tunes from a dozen songsters
hidden in the morning shadows of the willow oak.
They are not shy about their true message
in a muddled world.

It shows itself in the mysteries of
what is yet to come in each morning's awakening
—around the edges of the schedule when
we wash the grit from our habit-stained eyes.

Side Show

While six monsters and gravediggers
performed their scripted parts
under the thick-trunked shade tree
near some red raspberries in the back yard,
four mockingbirds pirouetted
on the ridge caps
of neighboring tin and tile rooftops,
appearing to show an interest
in the dashing and chopping going on below,
in the wood-fenced yard.

I wonder where the mockingbirds perch now
—whether they are re-enacting last night's show
on someone else's rooftop,
or checking out weird human behavior
in some other back yard,
—or whether they are simply glad
to freely devour the raspberries once again,
red juice dripping from happy beaks.

That tree

was not rooted by the rivers of water
nor could it stand when Your breath
blew invincible from on high,
visible only in what you left behind:

A fallen maple crowned in spring laurel,
already home for starlings and finches,
was food for the downy and red-belly
now perched on upturned roots
with cocked heads and questioning eyes.

Once it was shade for shelling peas
and snapping beans as games and yarns
spun the hours on the east porch of our house
—a shelter for my Mickey and black Alex,
guards and greeters of the front door.

How swiftly you plucked up this,
the second of two giants that towered over the farmhouse,
both felled in one year, halting forever
the flights on that long rope swing
that let the young soar like fairies
among their leafy kingdoms,
leaving only a gaping hole.

The Big Rain

Lo, the gold-green brilliance
of the sun-swathed willow oak
adorns my window this morning
after buckets and barrels,
boatloads and barnsful of raindrops
spilled over boundaries of streets and cellars,
drop by drip for an entire week.

The children,
barefoot and brimming with giggles,
did not complain.
With blue swirly balls and pink balls,
they squealed and splashed away
the evening hours in driveway pools
until dinner or dusk called them home.

Though weary of the heaven's weeping,
a tinge of envy tugged within,
wishing I could abandon
the reserve of too many years
and romp with the children
in the rain.

Said

The river said what it always said after a slew of rain
as it slid into the stream of morning.
The river did not scare the doe,
its copper sides visible between leaves
where it stayed still
until it heard, in spite of the river's rushing,
a new step.

I took a slow curve and found it staring,
its sleek neck bent backward in a question mark.
When I said, "good morning!"
it sauntered out of sight on the leaf-strewn trail.
I followed, saw it stop, and said again, "good morning!"
Then it leapt into the laurels seaming the river.

My sojourn crossed the covered bridge
where simultaneous sightings startled me and
a squirrel sitting on the wooden sideboard of the bridge.
A gray streak disappeared onto the back side of a nearby tree.

"I'm sorry doe, I'm sorry squirrel," I said.

After the evening's spate of showers
I was glad the robins and the thrushes
did not cease their singing
no matter what I said.

Labor Day on Loft Mountain

The promise of peace
among the gracious canopy of locust and birch
was broken by
intermittent cries of infants unseen but heard
across low-lying green hedges of wine-berries,
shoe-string bushes, and honeysuckle vines;
the ongoing drone of a young father near us,
teaching his young son about the pitfalls of life,
the occasional yip of canines throughout the camp,
and the drunken midnight song of German youth
staggering to the nearby toilet.

Yet, my inner ear turned always
to the whispered talk of the trees overhead,
their conversations more compelling than all the din,
and more persistent,
carrying me finally into the depths
of a healing rest that my soul will carry
into whatever the next days hold.

Black Friday

A morning chill still lurks
in the shadows of emerald pines
while sun rays flash, shimmer, and wink at me
between stones tuning the burble and shurr
of Madison Run.

Only a few chickadees scold from hidden branches
while a raven's call echoes from the ravine,
and a pileated pecker parts the air with bladed wing.

Lobed and needled oak leaves
drift, swivel and swirl
from gray branches etched into the blue beyond,
one small sapling still clutching its crimson clusters
among the brittle browns fallen on the forest floor.

On this Friday,
far from the mashing crowds,
these are the wares I treasure.

Mattamuskeet

Nothing was heard,
and then, out of the mist came
the distant calls of fabled tundra swans that
mingled with tribbling and muttering ducks
in the middle of Lake Mattamuskeet
as coots dabbled and dived in the canal lakeside.
We welcomed this February music like warm sunbeams
enveloping a chilled world after winter rain.

Here, pintails flip their pointed tails straight up,
shovellers shovel for grub in the shallows,
mergansers raise their white flagged hoods,
and herons stand motionless as sticks on stilted feet
'til glimpses of little fish unhinge long necks for a swift catch.

In the cypress bog, silence erupts into high-pitched
uh-uh-weets and low-voiced harrumphs as
frogs escaped from peopled places
combine in a deafening choir
and just as suddenly are stilled to utter silence,
only to begin again when our shadows pass.

Meadowlarks, long vanished from the green
fields of my youth, still trill on grassy banks,
flash black V's on their golden breasts,
signaling "Victory" in this non-partisan paradise.

What Matters

What matters
is that just around the bend in the road
among the myriads of golden rosinweed
the doe grazes with her twins of spotted bronze
at the edge of the emerald wood.

What matters
is that through the leafy giants
I can still see the evening's haloed sun
sending its rays to silver the tall grasses
at the edge of the clearing on Lewis mountain.

What matters
is that the wood's silence is punctuated by
twitters and warbles, caws and chirs,
—that dusk awakens katydids,
first a few to tune the choir, and
then, the very air vibrates with harmony
while a few proclaim their individuality
all night through till at dawn we hear
only the fiddles of crickets.

What matters
is that my love shares the tent,
the symphony of silence,
the symphony of song,
of the varied tones and tunes
of each singer in the forest.

What matters
is that the morning sun rises
in orange purple robes
like a priest performing his ritual of grace
to let the living:
the just and unjust,
the hurried and harried,
the sorrowful and forsaken
all have another go at life
—a resurrection of sorts
into the possibility of understanding
what really matters.

A Bird

1.
makes of any space a park
—like the bird singing lustily in the willow oak
and the red maple of my back yard
the summer after my mother found her eternal rest,
and someone sent you, little wren, her favorite,
to give me solace in the empty silence.

2
A bird
stopped this woman walking on Lewis Mountain.
As my flashlight focused on a white valentine face,
wise dark eyes stared from a branch overhead,
watching for a dinner of moths and mice.

3
A bird
clutched the tip-top of the one evergreen
reaching to the fifth floor
where I ran to the window to see
what singer emits such cheering song in the Egyptian city
where I was bereft of the Shenandoah.

4
A different bird
wagged its slender tail beneath the lavender
in Kathleen's back yard in Germany in June,
after I had noted its absence
in the sand beside the sea in Port Said
where it had wagged its black and white tail in January.

5
I am not a bird,
but perhaps one day
my husband thought I was lovely as a bird
 when, soon after marriage,
we hiked the trail to South River Falls,
and I kept stopping long moments
to fix my binoculars on black and white warblers,
red starts, magnolia warblers, and wood thrushes
while he watched my face,
fascinated by my focus on
the singers he never knew
in his small-town Minnesota.

6
In the end -of- summer stillness
of our last night on Loft Mountain,
out of the underbrush came
the towhee's solo at evensong.

Showing Up

1
My mother loved the wren
—it's sassy outpouring among the house trees.
And faithful as the wren,
she showed up every morning
to dish out our security
fixing corn mush and eggs,
or oatmeal with raisins.
Like the wren, she showed up singing.

2
The wren is more faithful
in showing up every morning
than I, who sometimes
wrestle the night before sleep shackles
the restless roving of my mind and body,
and I get up late.

3
Long ago, little wren,
was it your cousin that showed up
like a winged lute to
instruct the strings of the shepherd
who dispersed the shadows
of an aging Saul
as your song still inspires me?

4
Where were you, little mite,
when the wind showed up,
 grabbed ancient trees
and flung them flat like
once strong men felled by death?
Did you, like King David, find shelter among stones
and rocks that shielded you
from the darts of destroyers?

5
Sometimes, after raging winds,
in the stunned silence,
the Spirit shows up, like the wren,
to birth a new song
into the washed world.

6
When Jesus showed up
walking on waves,
touching the untouchable,
multiplying crumbs and revealing his wounds,
he gave the kingdom of heaven
a new definition, just like the wren
lends my garden a new grace.

7
As the wren
shows up daily
to preside over his leafy kingdom,
so Lord, may I notice
when You show up
in the garden I make of my heart.

Museum Afterthoughts

How is one supposed to feel
sitting comfortably by the fire in
a vintage inn in Orange County
located 500,000 years, at least, from
the time therapods roamed in the soft lakebed
later covered with layers and layers of rock
quarried finally by mere men doing their daily work
on voracious machines to scrape out
their living from the tombs of the once mighty?
In these ancient deaths, we were innocent.

How should we feel to walk on paved, big-box lined streets
and drive by fenced fields once roamed by
tens of thousands of Powhatans, Manahoacs and their brothers
who lived fully, yet frugally, from the soil, trees, and rivers
brimming with beaver, sturgeon, oysters and all manner of
living things we have ceased to dream of because our
dreams of plenty are filled with dead things that suck
the marrow from the weak bones
of our bodies and imaginations?

Who will pay for the plagues we visited upon the land's rightful keepers
who were listening when God said: "take care of the garden I gave to you?"

And are the ghosts of battles some believed
were arranged by the rich to be fought by the poor
still hovering over the hills of Harpers Ferry,
Manasses, Petersburg, and New Market,
 where uncles killed nephews
and boys punished family friends
dressed in blue or gray
 for crossing the line of North or South?

I do not know these things, sitting as I am
in warmth and comfort.

But this I do know.
Native offspring still struggle to survive
on barren lands bereft of buffalo,
where dry canyons remain and hope has fled.
Our powerful still send our ignorant youth to exact blood
beyond our borders where we don't have to look at
the broken hearts and bones our bombs scatter
—sowing what cataclysmic revenge?

Perhaps it were better that we, like dinosaurs,
would fossilize while there is still time.

Of Words and Walls

In the musty dung heap
of an almost forgotten synagogue in dusty Cairo
the Word was found in tatters,
then pieced together by someone
who still carried in the cave of their heart
the knowledge of a God who had spoken
into the silence of the desert
where now the servants of Mohammed
ensure there is no silence
as mosques rise out of the sand.

From imposing minarets, robed imams
blare out punctual prayers
between sunrise and sunset
facing ancient monasteries
where followers of Saint Anthony and Saint Mark
attempt to find space to hear God speak
into the modern caves of emptiness in their souls.
Inside sandstone walls they plant red roses
watered by streams from age-old springs.

Who will win this war of words and walls?
We wait and pray that love and peace
will rise red and irresistible as the roses.

CPSIA information can be obtained
at www.ICGtesting.com
Printed in the USA
JSHW010908110220
4155JS00004B/13